Accidental Joy

a streak of poetry

Judith Austin Mills

Plain View Press   www.plainviewpress.net
1101 W 34th Street, Suite 404   Austin, TX 78705

Copyright © 2014 Judith Austin Mills. All rights reserved under International and Pan-American Copyright Conventions. No part of this book may be reproduced or distributed in any form or by any means, or stored in a data base or retrieval system, without written permission from the author. All rights, including electronic, are reserved by the author and publisher.

ISBN: 978-1-63210-001-6
Library of Congress Control Number: 2014937261

Cover art: *As Far As I've Gone*, 2009 by permission of Genie Maples
Cover design by Pam Knight

Other books by Judith Austin Mills
How Far Tomorrow, a historical novel set during the Texas Revolution, was published by Plain View Press in 2011.

Acknowledgments
　　Gratitude to the following publications for printing these poems:
14 as "d r e a m   a   b u n d l e" in *di-verse-city*, 2011
27 as "b r i e f   p e a c e" in *The Weary Blues*, Issue 5, 2014, A Dublin online arts journal
29 as "d i z z y" in *di-verse-city*, 2008
34 as "r e v e l a t i o n" in *di-verse-city*, 2007
54 as "on the far edge" in *di-verse-city*, 2012
62 as "z i g z a g g i n g" performed June 7, 2008 by vocalist Suzi Stern. The lines were set to an original jazz composition by the author's brother John Mills for *On the Edge of the Page: An Exploration of Music and Verse*.
68 as "a s t a r k   p r e m o n i t i o n" in *di-verse-city*, 2004
88 as "all this before good-bye" in *Best Austin Poetry*, 2011-2012
94 as "c r e e d" in *di-verse-city*, 2010

*for
danda
forever
wherever
she might
live*

Contents

when words alone will fill this peculiar emptiness   9

1	syllable	
2	perfect curl	
3	clue	
4	rising	
5	final stretch	
6	accidental joy	
7	circle of light	
8	chalk squares	
9	champion	
10	more than okay	
11	sister path	
12	easy	
13	laurels	
14	dream a bundle	
15	rest assured	
16	holy center	
17	voice within	
18	launch pad	
19	cool thing	
20	cliff	
21	later	
22	swagger	

to lift oneself from the grasp of gravity   33

23	pristine	
24	worse	
25	solitaire	
26	endangered	
27	brief peace	
28	wing-stretching	
29	dizzy	

30 round table
31 communion
32 popsicle
33 countdown
34 revelation
35 key of be
36 deliver
37 woolen coat
38 tempted
39 mud pie
40 pendulum
41 plateau
42 second chance
43 riveted
44 tune-shuffling
45 professionals
46 enlightenment
47 eyelids
48 flight
49 unceremonious

voice   soul   memory   on black and white wheels

50 riddle
51 helluva hurry
52 conundrum
53 kaleidoscope
54 on the far edge
55 word-strung
56 shaking heads
57 conventional oven
58 tomfoolery
59 ricochet
60 longevity
61 camelot
62 zigzagging

63   last ditch
64   daydream
65   all-night ride
66   gone
67   slanting ray
68   stark premonition
69   big-bang
70   peach fuzz
71   cold turkey
72   sans wings
73   drag racing

of passion for life that runs beyond the shallow grave

74   under a pebble
75   microchip
76   cyclical question
77   sandbox
78   pockets
79   inky colors
80   unfettered
81   risking far more
82   inexplicable
83   channel settings
84   a melody's lift
85   inner fire
86   reservoirs
87   spun
88   before goodbye
89   atlantis
90   abundance
91   small feet
92   fraction
93   glitches
94   creed
95   daily bread
96   softy

97	bell tower
98	butterfly
99	bequeathed
100	page-long
101	kindred

About the Author	119
About the Artist	119
Gratitude	120

when words alone

will fill this

peculiar emptiness

1   *syllable*

if i am asked
what i intended
i will utter
the syllable
p e a c e
  for a great-great-
grand-niece   on the eve
  of the twenty-second century

an ancient clipping of hope
from the late nineteen hundreds

not this
maddening twist of knotted sheets
the slap of insomnia
hurling me from my bed
  half-choked
  and groping in the dark
  for my pen
  in self-defense

2 perfect curl

here's where
the first delicious
wave of solitude
rolls down the darkened hallway
washing over *me*
who will not yearn for water
   far too wet
   and seldom without grit
   or obscured danger
who can
on the other hand
relish
the sensual chill
of silent corners
and humming shadow

here's where i listen
for the last storm stirring in my mind
the perfect curl
swelling from inarticulate shores

here's where i leap
to let the crashing
breakers
have their way with me

3 *clue*

in that last poem
  the one i never mailed
  the lines i never meant
  the words i never spoke
  the voice
    i never sent your way
you would have seen
an altogether
non-unique
phenomenon

the speaker looking
back
at nothing in particular
except the missing
moments
documented
one-by-one
or locked in couplet rhyme
without a key
or clue
as to whether
the lived
or
the imagined life
is close
  or any closer
to what's true

4 *rising*

from this day forward
a vow
to rediscover
what we would have
grown into
had we not been
(case in point)
a mere substantiating
piece of evidence
that we are
not what we are
but
what we fell into
  slid against
    bobbed amongst
  lost our will to
    counteract

from this day forward
let us rising
wake to breathe
touch and shape
that very stuff into
what would have been
had we had
  t i m e
if we could
only

just
as
if

5 *final stretch*

how unlikely
  consider
  the thin dime
  landing on its edge
to comprehend   both sides
in one expanse of this mortality
first wishing   no clutching
for some final stretch
of unencumbered day-to-day
 as for *my own grasp*
without hesitation
serve up that morning
when i might lunge
from the covers
for paint brush and mug
budge from the canvas   but once
for better light hum along with
or in the absence of radio
eat from a misshapen sandwich
folded in a paper towel
fling myself   at last
without shedding my clothes
  into bed
as my neighbors rise for work

and sleep like a puppy
no questions asked
or answers sought
  about the spinning dime
about the other side of time
when the rest of my days
are all my own

and all i can do
is ask   where   everybody   went

6 *accidental joy*

without climbing
into the car
i can tell you how i'd take in
  upon arriving
the depth of quiet
in a forest's edge
  an eight-hour drive
  from here
or without contacting
tour planners   guides
what i would glean
eyes closed   palms up
in the secret caves
   of india
by the cloister turrets
   of tibet
at the six-inch differential space
 before one steps onto
 the dark side of the moon
  or the spot
   for that matter
where the wall in berlin   used to stand

tears with a new name
and more
for everything
endured and holy
random and glorious
for accidental joy
like brilliant filigree
spun
from my in-boxes
and your bar codes
to the far reaches
of the cosmos

7 *circle of light*

it is no matter
  nothing
    that merits complaint
that days lack perfection
that i am no more
a saint
than a day-glo
tyrant
that my achievement
climbs
to the elemental   grandeur
of pipe-cleaner
bas-relief
on a shoebox top
it is not
that i expected
    except on a covered porch
    in binghamton
    while rehearsing
    for princess
    in the second-grade play
a circle of light
floating in a darkened
sea

frustration is universal
small failures
  ubiquitous
terror as common as
house flies and colds

t h a n k s   g i v i n g
one midday meal
out of a commanding
three sixty-five

Judith Austin Mills

8   *chalk squares*

what i miss   most
are the carousel seasons
the clear sense
of purpose   in a strand
of squawking geese
maple leaves crunching
underneath leather oxfords
chestnuts crouching
in the pockets of coats
spirited tulips   and wild-card crocus
their dazzling liftoff through a powder of snow
street tag   hide and seek
red light   green light   star light   moon light
robbers and good guys   bad guys and cops
dibs   time out   i call   all-ee-in-free
thumb gum and baseball cards
cavanaugh's deli down the street
marbles for a quarter at the five-and-ten
this week's friendly fountain specials
double squirt cherry vanilla phosphates
cheese grilled flat as a greeting card
sky king lunch boxes
chalk squares on concrete
sawdust in basements
wooden planks winding
toward the perch in the tree

to see what you could see
which was
everything   e v e r y w h e r e
the perfect sum
of childhood   clicking off
its total
in the blink of
i am i

9 champion

what
we have
we have forgotten

but
i should speak for myself
before
i am called on the carpet
to explain
the evidence
in time chart inconsistencies
of the desk key lost behind a shelf
from the peeling i.d. or the frozen screen
amongst chalk dust and paper clip potpourri
to justify the
 hole punch confetti
 jammed drawer
 odd fork   the
   phone number   on the post-it
     without   a   name

i have forgotten
what first trespassed my mind
upon coming to consciousness
the undaunted
conviction
that i could
part uncharted seas
champion the sun's chariot
or fly with cardboard and tin foil wings
wherever whatever it took
to get to

where i have forgotten
to speak for myself

10   *more than okay*

    for this opportunity
    in all earnestness
    no tongue-in-cheek
    double entendre
    esoteric allusion
    or inside joke
    this chance to let you know
    that i see
      how hard it must have been
      to put up with
      me   past my colic infancy
        (i always assumed
          the second and third word
          being *no* as well)
      the crayon scrawlings on the wall
      playhouse stuffings under the bed
    was there anything like anxiety
    creeping dread   as i approached
    that pomp and passage across a stage
    eighteen years later
    and hijacked a flying carpet
    to whisk myself away   p o s t h a s t e
    to an inhospitable galaxy

    what i know now
    from a mother's eyes
    of self-reproach   and nail biting
    (that it might
    eventually come to this day
    not marked on the calendar
    or hawked in hallmark shops)
    did i ever tell you
    you were more than okay
    what colossal good fortune
    met my wailing debut

11   *sister path*

    if you were wondering
    whether i had managed   to say it   all
    if you were politely not asking
    how long this rash and fever could go on
    my letting free word upon phrase free fall
    splash onto these keys
        the answer is   *no*   *not late*
    yes   there are at least these verbal trickles more
    not on   *the house*   but   *houses*
    post-evolutionary technicolor dreams
    construction less of madness than they first seem
    chestnut street   for starters   three attic worlds
         dusty mattress boxes
       picture rowdy play   raw sweat
   room number two set for schoolmarm drama
    posturing with tablets at a pair of inkwell desks
      the final door   open   for solitary   serenades
        floating from a window without screens
    remember my third-floor quarters in grosse pointe
    a nanny's retreat in some parallel life
          claw-foot tub   *hers*   reclusive jumble   *mine*
     a ledge for a ladybug's funeral pyre
     past slumber that altar sill seeps to mind
           an overlook as inward   more private still

    there is   with your patience   this one furthermore
      for the road   s t e a l i n g   a w a y
    from behind the dusky house in natick   whether
    it even had an attic   my memory lines cannot recall
      but *oh*   the sister path of dirt and snow
    up a towering thicket slope   toward secret drinks
    at an enchanted pond where i could have just as easily
    drown   as flown wingless   and without eyes
    to each casement where i had never lived   nor will
    but have dared since to alight uninvited

12   *e a s y*

    i should have
    done this
       before
    next time
    i will
     what an easy thing to say
     all the while
     knowing
     how one day leads on to
     tomorrow
    with no button for
    replay

13   *laurels*

    this list of
    what i am *n o t*
    only grows
       no sitter
       no seamstress
       not a cook   of any kind
       neither housekeeper
       nor laundry girl
       nursemaid
       hostess
       whore
    and   don't ask me how
    but i have waylaid my looks
    where   god knows
    along the way   mind you   along with
    the self-doubt
    ingratiating disposition
    eagerness to please
    of the trophy wife
    it appears i've racked up
    an entire life   engaged
    in slow motion refusal
    of proverbial softer airs

    isn't it too bad
      too late
        (concentrate on *never*)
    that the demure answer
      no   did not give birth sooner
    don't ask me   *why now*   a parting nod
    or if it's due   to the fertile litany
    of laurels no longer within my destiny
    ringing in the front row
      prodigy l a t e b l o o m e r
        dear young thing

14 dream a bundle

if the rhythm don't
get you
or another reason kill
gotta
boogie-woogie life
with a passion
until
   the seasons bow out
until you ain't got *you*
or at least nuthin' like
what you used to see
gotta
shake a little shove a little
   — this can't be
claim the knees and the feet
i used to booga-looga-loo
barefoot in the street
to a lollipop moon
and a wild heartbeat
gotta
dance a bundle dream a bundle
   — that ain't me
say the sprites in the shadow
playin' sneak a peek
go look at yourself g i r l
   — what can this mean

if the count don't get you
and the rhyme don't die
as the spring holds still
  betta
  jambalaya
  NOW
or you never will

15   rest assured

may i
be the first
to acknowledge
that indiscretion
there
is
no forgiving
what
got into me
rest assured
the whim
has passed
and as you can see
i
have completely
recovered
my former
self
to check this out
you need only look
on   the middle shelf
  in the two-quart tupperware
  mold
next to
 the canister   of
  sleepy time tea
  bags

no
there is no
imperative
to inspect that
pulsating
parcel of
  costa   rica   java

16 holy center

i do
so want
to clarify
a statement made earlier
to   signify in a
less obscure way
what
i do
want to say
not just to family
friends
men
strangers
children
taken by the hand
treasured
needed
born
for a reason
i do
believe in
the holy center
where
breath
greets soul
i do

such meeting
is marriage
is birth too
 is
  are
  am
 is
i do

17 *voice within*

i have strayed
from my purpose
or taken one on
whereas
originally
previously
    (am i off track   again)
i was only listening
to the voice within
  i should confess
   my office skills are lacking
   filing and dictation
   as well as the rest
it is hard to say
when i am at
my best or worst
i only know
to write when i am hungry
when words alone
will fill
this
peculiar emptiness
soothe
this
unseemly
itching
assuage
this odd
thirst

18 launch pad

the age is n e w
and with a shred of luck
it is good news for
   them and me and you
our neighbors' offspring
and grandchildren
no longer
obliged to bear
stiffness of joints
or unraveling memory
inoperable pumps
or dimming sight   no more
invariable envy of flight
or yearning for youth
should our cares take off
like rising humidity
that disintegrates upon
cooling in the night
what will be left to
drag us down
we shall sprint
to the last flag
forever cheered on
spines unbent elastic skin
if not ecstatic
at least blissfully content
   u n l e s s
our luck weighs in the other way
wears itself thin
and we come to realize
that instinctive dread
was the launch pad for being
the loveliest part
of dying
after all

19 cool thing

      what they say about
        freedom
      the young ones
      well   we can all remember
        were all there at one time
      slicing the solar year into semesters
      what they say is they *w a n t*   it
      (that they can't use the other)
        yo f r e e d o m is
        that very cool thing
        we were wishing for now
        and not watered down fool
        we can taste the difference
      is what they swear
      though they haven't
      seen smelled heard touched
       sacrifice or rapture
       riot or renaissance
       the sublime or the sinister
      there is no surprise here
      the frayed but cocky edge
      of twilight innocence
      when the bars are lifted
      when at last you are permitted
      to range across the wilderness
      a   t e a c u p f u l
      meant to last a lifetime
      balanced on your head
        while you duck the odds
         dig for endurance
         sift for self-discipline
      as you would have once for g o l d
       and rejoice   if and when
       you manage   not to spill
       a drop

20 cliff

hush now   hush right up
don't you dare carry on thinking
you've conjured some
breakthrough infallible way
to calculate age as the function of youth
twelve times
a month of days
times black-eyed peas on
the soggy paper plate
at last new year's dinner
that little ole you
are the selected person to
stumble upon
one cumulative truth
from temporal
wisdom

hindsight
ought not to make a person brag
like a sheep bleating
on the way down from a sudden cliff
suggesting that
lambs on the sheltered slope
      are the real sinners
and
pretending to have
lived loving
a rocky demise
from the get-go

21   *later*

well
that's the end of that
if i sit long enough
i will have sat
through summer
as well
as spring
and though
i am most in love
with autumn
for its bawdy crackle
its boisterous fire
despite its wild reminder
that the thing called wind
  the savior of the seed
will sooner or later
bring around
the very first year
i am not *h e r e* for
  having gone
  where
i know i'll be invited
  as it were
  to a winter ball
  whether or not
  i have pictured it before
  have waltzed
  close enough   *thank you*
  with its skeletal trees
  have anything to wear
  or even want to go
  at all

22 swagger

if i can't have perpetual autumn
i will take
a surly spring
  like this one
first
spinning herself
dutifully
at the
fingertips of winter
into pear blossom lace
embroidered plum
and petticoat trees
then whipping
free from the diaphanous chain
  of command
to trounce
on subtlety
   tradition
   humility
   calm
to scoff in the face
of moderation
and swagger in
flagrant profusion
at
the last hint of
freeze

to lift oneself

from the grasp of gravity

23 *pristine*

when
they say *it is written*
you must step a pace back
reach for your spectacles
and verify
that on some other day
the headline
can't claim
it was *y o u*
your etched lack of
  spontaneity
    spunk
      verve
        wit
leaving page after page
so neatly stacked
pristine
aligned
and sadly blank

24   *worse*

there are metaphors
like spiritual rivers
   just as
life is a simile
   hoping death
is mere hyperbole
 rather than
 the personification
 of paradox
or
   (worse yet)
    the
     endless empty repetition
      of
        s u p e r f i c i a l   verse

25 *solitaire*

you should announce
to the critics
when you are having fun
lest your sport be mistaken
for
 c y n i c i s m
only somewhat less lonely than solitaire
but so much easier
  if not a cinch
to win

26 endangered

    if it is understood
      war is the essence of hell
      childhood at its worst is relative bliss
    how does one wee world
    sustain such robust soldiers
    conveniently miss the multitude of
      timid pleas— calls waiting—
      perpetually kept on hold
    if it goes without saying
      no man survives an island
      three invariably seem a crowd
    why the throng and circus uproar
      about who is holding hands with whom
        the arch and arbitrary exclusion of
        how we arrive at two's
    if it stands without question
      silence is honored treasure
      simple actions speak bolder than words
    what is the addictive attraction
    of this pitch.com din
    wherein lies the luster of brash deeds
      on sixty-minute fiction
        laughter canned by the half-hour
        seedy slugfest repartee
    if it lives undisputed
      age should precede allure
      blessings are wasted in our youth
    which door is at least being held open for
      the less glamorous   near anachronistic
      certainly   endangered species—

    integrity, charity, fortitude, forgiveness,
    gratitude, compassion, constancy, hope
    plainclothes kindness
    unadulterated old   truth

27 brief peace

sometimes
you have to lighten up
i did this once myself
and it paid off in ways
i am at a loss to measure
or capture
and that is the point
a chance to confess
i do not
    know what i am doing
a rare
pleasure
in and of itself
to forgo purpose
for a turn in the swing
out back by unfurling ferns
underneath the bradford pear
where a grackle pauses pointedly to
calculate his roost and breeding chances
before flapping obstreperously along
as if releasing me on my own
to observe branches quiver
and silvery sun shift
abandoning me
to brief peace
where
i no longer
    care what i know
where i wait nonetheless for
no one   rapt
and listening
for nothing more
than the next line
of this
s o n g

28   *wing-stretching*

lend   me   a lullaby

    a blue   rolling circle

bubble light   butterflies

    on blankets   of grass

float   me   through waterfalls

    of slow motion sundown

star glow   and marbled shade

    on green   hand-blown glass

sing   me   a fairytale

    by wing-stretching   m o r n i n g

gold dust   on gossamer

    for   amethyst   eyes

hold me   with arms of air

    and tresses   of summer

lift me up   melody   in absence of

    time   softer than   lavender

    dissolving at sunset   whisper

me   to a dream   where dark slumber lies

feather   touch   wakenings   with no ending yet

29 *dizzy*

when you snap your fingers
i will remember nothing
except that august morning
at auntie's farm
when i stood on the dirt road
in the neonatal sun
calling and clapping
as i was asked not to do
for the neighbors' punk dog
who came at a feverish gallop
and just as had just been
expressly forbidden
drove then cornered nervous sheep
in her red ohio barn
i will remember nothing
except the three-legged tomcat
ten thousand kittens
fluttering chickens in the pungent coop
the sprawling unfenced corn-fed yard
the city girl thrill
of imprisoning fireflies
fretful train-whistle sleeping
to the creaking of a pitched roof
the muffled call of bingo numbers
down an embankment of odd narrow stairs
where i stole upon dressing first at earliest light
seeking the cheerful kitchen
and finding her alone   smiling
looking down at me   in my expectancy
with moist and ancient eyes
great auntie ernestine
who had no babes of her own
but a minimalized childhood
best forgotten
visiting with equal wonder
a habitat of rambunctious beauty
and dizzy spinning joy
that she had never known

30 round table

    at least once   it went
    as it was meant to be
    a mother whose incandescence
    was not painted on
        as brilliant as forgiving
      as beautiful as fond
    loved and in love
    along with
    a father whose power
      welled from tenderness
    a fixer with a sense of humor
      a maker of music
        and magical play
    it went as it was meant to be
    together nightly
          at a round table
    three brothers   the two of them
      (thank the friendly stars) me
    summer treks and weekend excursions
    museum exhibits   picnics   nature walks
    fair rides   concerts   mountain campsites
    cross country songfests
    fireside talks   hide-the-thimble
    humming and hymnal sharing
    books   puzzles   jokes   blocks
    whimsical snacks   stuffed animals
    under tucked and snuggled-in
    familiar bedcovers kisses and prayers
    unabashed and going by
    as they were meant to be
    from the perfect grace
    of simple good will
    to   g o d
      and absolutely
    back

31 communion

why then
has the rest been
not remotely easy
nowhere close to *given*
why (is the question)
be so driven to take
the twisting route
such blistering trails
all roads incommunicado
every fragmenting precipice
any scorched stretch
each churning wave
  this shifting shore
is it that
i
could not accept
happiness
any more   without
understanding
its undertow
am still unable to
float blithely
flaunting satisfaction
as a queen parades a crown
until i plumb
the depths and learn
to drown as most people do
  quietly   alone
and without assigning blame
teaching myself
in the last seconds
to let communion
buoy my weight and offering
to the angels of gratitude
my name

32   *popsicle*

how the best dreams
trickle and merge
is like a wyoming stream
along an evening bike ride
after dinner and before
your idle bath
p e r c o l a t i n g   into
a ferry crossing
a ferris wheel
a slip 'n slide
or a blue pitcher
at a spigot
filling
and overflowing
mounds of
petunias
redolent
in its aftermath
with the velvet air
rushing
to your ears
through your salty hair
as if you were listening to
an unknown ocean
on   *e u r o p a*
in a
popsicle
shell

33 countdown

we pretend not to complain
about the passing of
seasons
   simply the pace
at one end
 of the spectrum
the incremental   turning
by squeaky seconds
of day after day   thumbing
through an impossible
slew of agenda pages
still-life and similar
no matter how illuminated
that never arrive
but to embark
on another round of inserts
   or the occasional insight
that it only gets worse
when your life
unlike light
learns to travel
in reverse and decades
sweep to a tidal
rush finish
sucking your history clean
like dross from the sand
back to the countdown
(all your very own)
to the moment time
took off
when you can only
gape at
the present
and cringe to ask
where tomorrow has flown

34 *revelation*

it remains in doubt
how to weigh in
and measure
the relative difference
between
sins of *nostalgia*
and *prognostication*
a dilemma
which leaves us
one slight and fleeting
yet certain revelation
that on any modern day
we are still
but gatherers of grain
or hunters
   either flinging seeds
   that speak to us of
   past harvest
   and seduce us to romanticize
   rewards long vanished
or (for better or worse) *the other*
   tensed and crouching
   among mobile shadows
   in ignorance of
   the bounty at hand
   as we steal up
   on uncertain advantage
   in the yet-to-come
   as one would track
   an elusive
   and immortal prey

35 *key of be*

what makes us so unwilling
to dance with living in the here and now
to serenade life in the key of *be*
to pluck our *b e i n g*
   humbly   like a homely fig as it ripens
   on an everyday tree

is it blessing or curse
this thing *i m a g i n a t i o n*
that can paint purple birds
   on their flight into a chartreuse sun
arouse the spirits of ancestors
and bid them run with
teeming herds of unicorns
or swim with mermaids
where a rising fresco stream
pours over gilded banks
and turns a great desert into
 shangri-la

without such fancy
we should see life as it is
embrace   finite
   r e a l i t y   permit *immediacy*
the spare nobility it achieves
   among nature's other   creatures

who ever heard of
a lovelorn polar bear
fashioning a taj mahal
from arctic ice
or a ferret named adam
extending a forepaw
toward
the outstretched hand of god

36 deliver

such paradox and irony
that start to mix and intertwine
deliver simultaneously
some ageless universal
and what
(in all modesty)
remains exclusively
mine

and
that
i surmise
is the nature of art
any hidden doorway
unlikely few are likely
to seek out
yet once unlocked
or pried ajar
opens to the multitudes
onto a
native path of
unmuddied colors
and primary syllables
orchestrating
for at least a second time around
the frank exhilaration
in a purposeful step
while intimating
a way to talk
without camouflaging
our souls

37 woolen coat

this lucky recollection
    one   dream-of-a-kind
 (never mind the recurring
  community nightmares
   both incidental and grandiose
    spawning tornadoes
    spaghetti overpasses
    melting rubber bridges
    unhinged steering wheels
    crumbling bicuspids
    public fuzzy slippers
    counter-wise clocks
    awol clothing   warning bells
    lost objectives   evaluators
     on task and busy
     marking *zero*

never mind   these silly collective twitches
or politically correct disdain
for a woman's graces)

  oh most private   white christmas   reverie
    my mother and i in a wintry boston car
    no holy snowflakes
    on her plain woolen coat or mine
    alike to any prodigious degree
    even our frosty impulse corsages
    more clashing than in harmony
    the bright mirror sphere
    in the center of hers
    reflecting nevertheless
    my adoring gaze
     mine managing to capture
     the admiration
     of an archangel

38 *tempted*

it should be winter
that makes a person weep
 the absence of leaves
 the dearth of color
 the flight of song
 the chill in a norther
what could there be
 in green determination
 in gutsy cacophony
 and roiling *joie de vivre*
to make me bow my head
for forgiveness
    in prayer
    and some despondency

the unembellished
confession
that
(were it left just to me)
i might not muster
such exquisite energy
i might be tempted
to let the
frozen ruin rule
if only to claim
more effortlessly afterward
that i'd had a hand
in
something

39 *mud pie*

this takes me back
to a magnificent mud pie
i once created
from an ingenious mélange
of garden dirt and sandbox grit
the objet d'art
  had i been so equipped
  to judge it then
was
(to say the very least)
of *louvre* quality
i cleverly hid it   under my bed
guarded it   *yea* more jealously
than the underground
that prevented   *mona lisa*
from resurfacing post-war
as a lunatic nazi

and this concrete brilliance is not all
  only a beginning
nay   i have produced   have i not
stapled hems   rock-hard brownies
glued stuck birthday cards
bald dollies   strung macaroni   kitten bottles
useless but colorful cloth-covered baskets of
  yarn-looped   hand-dyed and sequined   s t u f f
to recall but a few unorthodox gems
all accepted and discreetly discarded
handily enough   but without proper appreciation
for what it takes   *i'll warrant*
to demonstrate past all doubt   r e i n c a r n a t i o n
  as the reborn inventor of the rustic wheel

the lass for whom recipes and rules proved horrific
when i'm gone may they prize all my junk as prolific

40 *pendulum*

to certified intellectuals
   (the caustic   and with all respect due
   whomever else it concerns)
do you find
as connoisseurs of
fine wine and philosophy
that undistilled humor
cleanses the palate
or does it leave you
ho-hum
do you much prefer
to let the
critical pendulum swing
as wide as it will
past its balance
at centric
calm
before its
most deeply cutting and
inevitable return
where it is
to you
of idle import
whom or how many
it rends
or that
there is
precious little
other
earthly
balm

41 *plateau*

when at last
you accomplish fifty
you may say
you have arrived
and it's best you do
rather than attend
the others
who are either
  young or
    languishing in
    a state of stunned disbelief
     or have already achieved
     what you barely dare
     imagine

    the next plateau

      physical perfection
      postmortem wisdom
      uninterrupted relief

42 second chance

some think
we have all been here before
me too
the trail   the pace   the fixed direction
all uncannily familiar
even the names
begin to ring their own bells
and the faces   without question
i recall seeing yours
on a previous occasion
though your eyes
at that time may have been
half-closed
your nose   was it maybe
more arched or flared
you were possibly taller
wider   hunched   more muscled
red-headed   albino   or raven-haired
i think i remember an exotic tongue
neither eastern   nor slavic   nor latin-based
issuing from your full pouting lips
or were they pursed   near invisible
the same hue as your skin
certain specifics escape me
though
i so clearly remember the shape you were in
doubtful   wistful   pressed for time
while   yearning for a second chance
we were all there   racing to the faux finish
   brothers   and   sisters
observing keenly each other and ourselves
assessing such differences in minute detail
  letting identical toddler souls
  lag behind   without so much
  as   a   backward   glance

43 riveted

i have been to england
it was strange to see
how the odd-chance endless stretching
of solid blue sky   could transport
without exception
an entire population
into a mood of mirth
  quintessential good cheer
  without boundary
while for those of us in texas
as from   dry gulch
the outback   badlands
or central sahara
it is the quixotic formation
of a single gray cloud
or lone drop of h2o
that so uniformly
sends us

in the tropics perhaps there's
a snowflake preserved
in some hospital's deep freeze
to extract only   in case of
  emergency malaise

it makes one wonder
(or maybe just me)   if there isn't
shuttling toward us from across the
  airless   weatherless   galaxies
a troupe of avant-garde travelers
that will be   riveted   uplifted   bowled over
upon their arrival here   by our
  (how shall we characterize
  the customary disposition of the species)
f r e n e t i c   c o m p l a c e n c y

44 tune-shuffling

the mood may be precisely right
for   another soothing   b a l l a d

when dogma or didacticism
worms its way into your lines
it is time to cut bait
as we metaphorical fishers say

i am with you
i'd as soon
strap myself to
a sinking submarine or
the backside of the moon
as enlist for yet another
lecture series
self-help get-ahead just-for-dolts   how-to
all-you-need simon-says starting-off who's-okay
make-the-most gotta-do must-believe-guru

(number one
 two-hundred-forty-seven-days-in-a-row
 consecutively and counting
 nationwide bestseller
 you can't go wrong with that)

when a single small-print axiom
                    is as obvious as it is free

consider life-altering choices
  no less deliberately
  than a tune-shuffling d.j.
     or   as your least accommodating
     colleague consciously
     picks over options
     for a lunch buffet   s a l a d

45 *professionals*

don't turn that dial
you must not think you've been forgot
if you were waiting for something
more airy
and light
    all spiritual things
    in their own ephemeral
    time
and so
without
any further
 tah-doo
let us
hold hands
hum the pitch
set a rhythm
eye *the conductor*
wait conscientiously
(like the professionals we are)
for *his or her*
cue
and
s—i—n—g
(you heard me)
as if
there were
no other
way to convey
the primordial message in
our contemporary hearts
as if
  all this talk had
  not yet been
  invented   or then ordained as
  n e c e s s a r y

enlightenment

if what constitutes heaven
is not this
what is

could there be
greater pleasure
than to
say
without sound
the stray
but welcome
however sparse
enlightenment
that's been
floating around
in your brain
since the day
you were born

47 *eyelids*

speaking of which
i can't seem
to pin down that initial
recollection
i am able to remove myself
from the   n o w
temporarily
and retrace
with some success
last year
past decades
even adolescence
childhood   then one
  notch less
  is where
  it gets rough
there must
have been
such hopeful faces
hovering intently over
mine
waiting attentively
  for my *windows to the soul*
  to open
i was probably
playing *real-good-possum* inside
or drawing *cheerios*
on the backs
of my
eyelids
hiding
waiting
for any lapse
in their inspiration
before tiptoeing out

48 flight

    we see far much too much
        written about birds
      in my opinion
the debate
about whether
there's a link
to the dinosaur
      is moot
they are here
as are we
both of us
technically free to pursue mates
and perches   so to speak
we have two legs
  at the end of
  whatever they call
  their own
  they too have two feet
this much comparison
meets with my
approval
could we please
get over now
the impulse
for rank sentimentality
about their power
of flight

  as if the ability
  to lift oneself from
  the grasp of gravity
  were tantamount to
    simultaneous
    transmogrifying frolic and
    no-frills resurrection

49   *unceremonious*

when all this is over
and no incarnation goes on
forever
(rest assured
there is nothing
like the written word
so rapidly
on its way
to a quiet
unceremonious close)
to rephrase
when these print-bytes of mine
  so sputtering
  and effete
end   same as the rest
that is
conclude dripping   go kaput
dry up   shrivel to a stop
  (you may be thinking
    mercifully just   cease)
please
consider
the environment
and dispose of them
where they can decompose
and be recycled
at least as an insignificantly minuscule patch
in the ozone hole
or at best
  as   one
  millisecond of chimerical release
  for an eight-year-old
  malaysian girl
  who went to sleep
  after a twelve-hour
  work day
  believing
  she was alone

voice   soul   memory

on black and white wheels

50 riddle

i am not much
for record keeping
though it affords
me no small pride
to say i haven't bounced
a check in ages
furthermore
the documentation of
my self-improvement
   like refinancing
   and warranty upkeep
has been decluttered in
incremental stages
that i think are
looked upon with
favor by experts in the field of
image makeover
i'll be damned
(first take intended)
if i should claim
that i now
live day-to-day
free of sin
(however i can swear on
 any testament you choose
 that currently i own far better standing than
 the sorry shuddering shape i was in
 before deducing what *not* to do)

all that leaves me
(and i admit to being
  past the halfway point)
is the task of solving the riddle
about going straightaway to hell
on the light rails of *good intent*

51 helluva hurry

a sage is seldom
recognized
on home turf

this disturbing
factoid
could explain
why
just the other day
while on my way
to the jiffy mart
i was mistaken
for
a flabby middle-aged
pre-retirement
school teacher
shabbily dressed
and apparently
in a helluva
hurry
to snatch up
a handful
of nutty buddies
and make it
back to
the lazy-boy
before
starting seconds of a
seinfeld rerun
and the ice cream
meltdown
  (or doomsday
  whichever
  might have happened
  first)

52 *conundrum*

there is *w-o-r-k* to be done
as always
alas
there's no
laureate prize
in the wings waiting
for the
most poetic
articulation of
   the existence
   antithetical
  or *the drudgery*
     conundrum

(you know)

what probably
to start with
got cain and abel
into such a
serious snit
 as if *it* were
    anybody's fault

how
that very thing
you must ever do
to survive
is the same thing
preventing
you
from l i v i n g
    as well as from believing
  that you are
  alive

53 kaleidoscope

poems present themselves
as paintings do
to me
you might picture how i meet
the shapes and moving
colors that nudge themselves
onto the empty screen
first stealing timidly
surreptitiously
along the edges
where they greet each other
and make friends with blank spaces
   like invisible notes from
   an unwritten symphony
   composing its own movements
then daring themselves
into full natural light
as kaleidoscope memories
one canvas layer
after another
materializing and mingling
for anyone so inclined
to hold and turn and see
collages and close-ups
of   dreamscapes
   spirit portraits
   minimalist washes
   keepsake reality
in shades
i had never
thought to mix
before

54 on the far edge

somewhere in georgia
(i could locate a *triple-a* road map
but by this time tomorrow   the official real-time
coordinates would escape my supra-perfect memory)
  within the certified boundaries
  of this red-dirt-part-of-a-whole   is the state of mind
  i would select had i any power over perpetuity
  how this designation came about
  is either second nature or impossible to grasp
  depending on your own perception
   of   paradise   eden   heaven   nirvana

it was there i could embark on two naked feet
having left my steaming sneakers on the warm gray steps
of my soft-spoken grandmother's
   broad wooden porch   to light out past the neighbors
down the buckling grass-stuck rain-cooled sidewalk
beyond the piggly wiggly   to the courthouse corner
where it was just as inviting to choose   left   as right
meander toward the pharmacy and beauty parlor
or the matinee posters at the fifty-cent movie theater
to visit grandpa's local hardware off the beaten path
ending up in the dime store for the annual summer
    blow-your-own-plastic-balloon-globs-on-a-straw
purchase   saving nickels for a raspberry push-up
all gone but the last melting bites upon return arrival
in their backyard swings   near the grapevine arbors by
the tantalizing toolshed at the vegetable garden off the
freestanding garage   on the end of the sand-and-pebble
 driveway   next to the aromatic kumquat tree   where
two of us   just my older brother and me   knew
      somehow   instinctively   that
  we   f l i c k e r e d   then
    on the far edge   of the unexplored universe
     or the elysian fields   and
as close to home as a human of any age ever gets

55   *word-strung*

    before this
     oddball effort
    i was under the impression
    foolishly and falsely
     apparently
      obviously
    that
    poetry
    of necessity
    was
    one unique
    memorabilia thing
    or another
    instead of
     any
     word-strung
     individual's
     modest memoir
     of positively all
     that has
     happened
     to each
     of us

56   *shaking heads*

      i may at this juncture
      be out on
      a so-called   limb
      i cannot see
      the shaking heads
       but
         i can sense them

      i may have taken
      into my mouth
      more words than
      i can eschew

      it's because
      i can't keep
      the thoughts
      i eat
      that i'm
      offering
      so many
      to you

57 conventional oven

i'm fond of cooking up that sort of thing
mashing a thick dollop of profundity
in between two thin
layers of
anything semi-sweet
then placing the dubious
concoction
in a conventional oven
of moderate
heat
and
watching
the timer

(which i
invariably
neglect to set
so that
i remain
oblivious
as to whether
anything
ever gets
done)

58 tomfoolery

very late at night

(the digital indicator reading
just 10:35 appears *without question*
due to the heinous tomfoolery
of a virus-drunk hacker)

so late at night   so serenely alone

(i anticipate another unsolicited
 software sales appeal)

i   plot   to commit
unnatural acts

(the renaissance has
ended in a bear market
 and few of us were there
  for the *last hurrah)*

i am the foul
perpetrator of the very worst
victimless   crime

(the handful who
truly know my voice
  are already in awe
   that i have refrained
from my customarily
shitty word choice)

with help from no
assistant   in   the audience
  i detonate
   yet another *rhyme*

59 ricochet

just outside my study window
a simmering spring storm is
coming to a full boil
making those of us inside
wonder
whether there will be gusty winds
or just fat drops of pelting rain
or if all-hell hail will ricochet
from the rooftops to the
nursery tree limbs
cradling their wards
of infant green
and bounce or crash against
the thin protective panes
precariously placed between
some of the most fragile
flowers in *the big picture*
and the senior engineers of nature
who still aren't much worried
about
how to work us
into their equation

60 longevity

when i am done with this
i had better remember
to look both ways
to carry an umbrella
to get plenty of sleep
to eat my fruit and vegetables
to take along a sweater
to hold as close
as i dare
without threatening to smother
my father and mother
my children
my brothers
their wives and daughters
my best-friend husband
and a few kindred kind
who would mind
my absence

such transcendent
joy
as power of expression
now permits me to feel
that i question whether
original
low-interest
longevity
is any longer
part of
the deal

61   *camelot*

those gone too soon
should long be remembered
i once cherished a preacher whose farewell sermon
was also a chance to hug earth
goodbye   his fond benediction
was not long after the *prince of camelot*
kissed the sky   then   a peaceful king murdered
and an idealist brother   while a non-war scissored
down to size a burgeoning but naïve generation
and it's as hard to account fully for the soulful genius
     lost to   erratic   self-medication
   peace-lovers   riff-players   neighbor-healers
     freedom-savers   change-makers   art-shakers
  speech-shapers   watch-keepers   risk-takers
     bright-shiners   life-givers   all
       all honored and mourned and honored more

you would think such loss
learned along the same years
as steering past sudden hazards and shifting gears
     would prepare the callow driver
         for nasty curves coming later   however
i could not keep tears from future wrenching news
  the neighborhood boy   whose neck snapped in play
  a virtual sister   lost to waterlogged lungs
  two innocent strangers   locked in a sinking car

it makes me want to ask the one too sad to name
if there were any lone reflections upon drifting away
if a last wish came to *you*   (unlike all the others)
    that you had *somewhat* lived   before you died
the lord lift up his countenance upon you
just the same   and may my own date of expiration
     shame me from tossing   anything like despair
     out on our only road

62 *zigzagging*

on our own
it turns out
   we are not able to fly
at best
on a gray day
we can let ourselves
drive in the direction
of the nearest low-key
inner-city intersection
where we won't have
to wait
for more than one changing light
before following the thoroughfare
roughly a country mile
z i g z a g g i n g purposefully
through the last of the
synchronized subdivisions
p e r s e v e r i n g
checking dials gears gauges
   rearview mirrors
for what might be approaching
then finding a four-second window
where we can afford to ease
a foot off the gas pedal
lift our gaze from the pavement
and   steal any reassuring vision

maybe something like
   a hawk rising up from a twisted oak
   catching an ascending breeze
   and turning aside on one wing
   with its eyes closed

63 last ditch

to tire entirely is human
to fly away is divine

what
appeals
to us
terribly
what drives this
non-stop fantasy is
the notion
that with wings we
could extend
(*just this once   sweet jesus*)
our sorry last ditch energy
no farther than the
tips of our fingers
flap our arms not an inch beyond
our own simple but complete embrace
(g l o r y be)
and by doing so
    abandon
    (a-a-a m e n)
to   its   ever-luvin'   destruction
 o u r
twenty-six-hours-a-day-eight-stints-a-week-
caffeine-guzzling-stress-belching-ass-whipping-
adrenalin-sucking-soul-snuffing-pep-zapping-
beast-bashing-smaller-beast-
go-gettum-and-i-mean-before-you—g-e-t—g-o-t

lifestyle
(h a l l e l u j a h)
like   so much
spinning dust fluff
downwind of a
meteor shower

64 *daydream*

from within this windowless room
off the middle hallway
inside
our
fortified
two-story
public
structure
those of us
left
without
library permits
daydream of pages
turned by a sudden
burst of wind
and
write
by hand
(if we remember
how)
the words
  b l u e
and
        s k y
  and
            l i b e r t y
  and
                  u s e d   t o

65 all-night ride

while i say nostalgia is a sin
i will still reach past i will always
wander in where my heart thump
commanded more than current faint thrums
in my very weakest moments   i would
trade most any   *now*   for those surreal drums
like the night my floppy hat got left behind
at a curving booth in the college commons
and though i hurried back to search the fair
such shades and heads
in every shape were everywhere
that if my felt chapeau still lay in sight
i did not care that i did not care
if the soft brown thing had stretched itself
into yet something else even farther out
atop the as-long-as-loosened hair
of another virtually bare breast girl
her own green-blue-green gathered skirt
brushing the gently bending floor
gliding her way out an imagined door
to a glowing rainbow flower box van
pulling off at an overlook on the edge of town
while french coffee drips
from a paper-towel filter
and over the radio an electric pulse throbs
from a solo needle digging vinyl
before the all-night ride to santa fe   where
an ocean of smoke swirls above a peacock stage
makes a *give-it-to-me* sea surge to sweep the fifties
from their sock-hop feet and their skittish piety
washing way off and warding away
three benign decades through the not-now nineties
for another thirty years i might believe
she was never me
                          (but oh was i ever there)

66 gone

you see why
you must
tread lightly
out the sacred back door
why you must not
stroll too far
you will only
want more
you will secretly
regret
that you must
come right in
from play
while
whatever
made you
hunger once
to arrive at last
   inside
you will
remember
to forget
in case
   what's
   gone
   is
   not   gone   yet

67   slanting ray

don't leave
please   just stay for a while
if i haven't made you groan too much
or caused a smile however weak
to tweak the corners of your mouth
it could be that
another of these
   pop-tart lines
   wobbly refrains
   strange sonatas
   sideways windows
will better weather
stamina and standards

would it mitigate to know
i need your tender ears
as i do mine
that my meager sight
grows strong
when you see
as if new   what you believe
while i sing-song what i must mean
does any interest mount
to take me at my feral word
   i refuse bitterness
   only that
   it has bitten your heart
   as into my own
   i have sat next to peace
   ever since you
   reached for
   warmth
   and touched but one
     slanting ray
      of comfort

68 stark premonition

we all know what it is
to see the blackened
sky at night
light up beyond the wit
of artificial day
to behold the backdrop
break apart with jaw-dropping
brain-stopping
earth-born energy
how before our hearts
can fumble for their pace
the crowning thunder booms
and rumbles through our bones
then
  all goes dark
from deep freeze lights to stereos
from kitchen clocks to videos
and noiseless absence reigns
       (save telephones)
no humming thermostat   or sizzling lamp
electric zing of this and that
just curious and self-conscious breathing
small coughs for odd embarrassment
blunt reminders of bygone ways
of hands-and-knees crawl-on m i l l e n n i a
and a stark premonition
of the greater streak of silence
lurking   still   just off the radar screen

69 big-bang

    if life were a trek
    we took for one week
    however level
    and planned
    we would stop
    along the way
    to feel the air inflate our lungs
    to dip our toes into a creek
    to taste existence
    with our tongues
    to sit somewhat still
    for at least the time it takes
    to believe
    as if newly discovered
    that the earth
    spins and circles
    neither to spite nor appease our will
        we would find such time
        if we lived but a day

    that being the case
    as earth's sons and daughters
    we might as well
        r e l i s h
    green wind   rippling water
    before a stampede in the planetarium
    before renegade moons kamikaze mad stars
    before their next
    crash pad
    big-bang
    all-night party
    laced with otherworldly creative highs
    or our cataclysm

70 peach fuzz

there are beacons
to behold
but they don't shine sweeping out
like a towering light from shore
their beams don't search for us
nor we them any more
so who is to say
how we
stay on swerving course
paddling away from
low-grade fever doubts
catching forward currents
whenever we may
what are the odds
that the offspring of remorse
will send any signals
to guide our way

today a human cherub
in peach fuzz overalls
touched her small-fry fingers upon my knee
she was one
she was free
she was walking radiance
among greenhouse flowers
if i close my eyes
and hold her smile
as it followed me
i will see again
where such beauty leads
i will
i believe
i will see

71   cold turkey

b e w a r e

poetry
is no plaything

it is not for children
to handle unchaperoned at home

even the heimlich-trained adult
proceeds at risk alone

writing without directions
t a k e s
a   lot   out   of   you

if you speak of
where you go
  it scrapes the soles from your feet
if you tell
what you have lost
  it steals an up heartbeat
to write
what you might know
    exacts a thin slice of brain
to hint
what is in store
    zonks your eyeballs with strain
if you guess
what people need
  the air is sucked from every pore

but if you quit
don't go cold turkey
less and less will cure you more
  a hideous withdrawal
  could leave you
     mute   like   before

72   *sans wings*

did you suppose
those lines were my last
that i would part company
on predictable rhythms
and wholesome end rhymes
did you figure
i would let this airborne volume
come in for a soft landing
or crash comfortably
on the cushion   of a major key
   relax and put your feet up
    i may arrive early
     but i am loath to leave on time

besides   i'll share a secret
that you haven't asked to know
i am only jotting down
  what   d a n d a   says to
    the voice of my childhood
    imaginary friend
(this is restricted information
but i choose to let you in
for my own protection later
if not for higher cause
i am no joan of arc
i could no more bring myself
to claim connection to the gods
than i could barter off the folks i love
for a cool breeze in july)
    shaman   prophet   martyr
    i am
    none of these
    nor an angel sans wings
    nor even nightingale
just a sedentary lark

73 drag racing

c o f f e e
(if you were wondering
　what i must be on
　　　good stuff　only half
　　　　well sifted with decaf)
i need no other inebriant
than the starting line of the next novel
　or a story title　　or the first words of
　　a newly christened　character
or a musical juxtaposition
ripe enough with
possibility
that it may linger
as long
as a culminating chapter
before it finds its
nesting syllables
　if this is intoxication
　it is near-holy frenzy
　it is the parable of the talents
　in a pop-up book
　　holographic
　　　yin-yang
　　　　neo-neurotic
　　　3-d
i write because i cannot
　will myself to break
　from this addiction
i am in love with
　the slender lyrics
　drag racing through my mind

voice　soul　memory
　on black and white wheels
　　　their　momentum　driving　me

of passion for life

that runs beyond the shallow grave

74 under a pebble

i am nearing the end
it is not yet in sight
      (not   q u i t e)
but i am starting
to laugh
to keep from crying
i would not be lying if i said
i have taken on too much again
and overshot my mouth
    (note to self
       make room here
       for another bird analogy
         not the one without wings
           the one too silly to flounder south
           after the first biting frost)

i would like to lie down
    in soft kentucky grass
   watch a green beetle
    slip under a pebble
and find rest
   as though it were
    never lost

75 microchip

    we fools move
        too fast
    we live as if
      the spirit
      were a
      mercurial
      microchip

    we pillage the day
    as if our bodies
    were the ruling pharaohs
      of the cosmos
    as if they were buttressed
      by the grand wizards
      of architecture
    programmed to run the life span
    of the vast primeval nile
    as if they were the part of ourselves
    destined
    to last

76   *cyclical question*

i keep looking ahead
to get to a place
where i have been before
any of
several spots in time
would do

the massive mountain rocks
my brother and i
sat among
while a chilly stream
swept around us from its secret source
to the far-off measureless mix of salty pools

the fussed over sheets
i stretched upon
when smiling attendants first brought in
my bonny baby   and laid him
clucking at my breast

the surreal roomful of strangers
where i sat reciting silent prayers
(can it be twenty years ago)
and as i turned to view new faces
on the workforce scene   saw *you*
so distant   and so *there*
then felt the cyclical question
intercede

must it be thus
  must one
  p r o c e e d
  stumbling along these jagged trails
    in every intangible way
    alone

77 *s a n d b o x*

we have told one another
that we should have met
sooner   not when others might think
(not on the rebound of the last divorce
or the eve of the very first starry nuptials
    or virgin intercourse   well before that)

we two ought to have met
long before the days of
drive-in movies and root-beer floats
of homecoming mums
and marathon phone calls
or drooping bouquets and groping dances
chiclets   cherry cokes   half-time shows
english leather and *right guard*
aqua-net and *white shoulders*
or awkward promenades in the mall

even before the swapping of homework
giggling in lunch lines   little league
passing notes   spin-the-bottle
valentines

we confide in each another
that we should have met ages ago
  in a sandbox
  with a canopy
  one shiny pail
  two shovels
  zero protocol
    (i would have been tickled
    to witness you spilling clumps onto your foot
     you would have taken on
     the dunes of alamogordo
     to laugh as i conversed with my toes)

78 *pockets*

along the way
i have had some serious friends
who advised me
(with nothing but lovely intentions)
to beware
of too much laughter
let it not be
all you run after
they warned
in an effort
to keep me from
falling in with jolly thieves

they did not know
such sorrow had filled my pockets
that no joy
lightening me
could ever be too much

79 inky colors

if admitting
my intimacy with
dark undercurrents
sounded   anything like a complaint
let me move quickly on
to say i would not want
to dogpaddle   in a calm
protected bay   all my life
i cannot paint with greens and blues
squeezed neatly from their tubes
they must be mixed with browns and grays
and muted hues
to keep my soul afloat
i have touched down
on the silty terror at the bottom
so that i might push up from instinct
instead of sight
i feel no more dissatisfaction in my skin
than a black swan bemoans its lack of flight
i love to dip my brush in inky colors
i plunge headfirst into swirling contrast
even though i fear deep water
even though i cannot swim

80 unfettered

teach me
to revere
the hairpin turn of fate
that dealt such
choice my way

to abhor
the grating confines
countless others
rub against
at every breath

remind me
that freedom
conceives itself   and then
gives birth to eternity

when i speak
let me
honor unfettered articulation
with an imperfect   but familial
and fearless
voice

81 risking far more

of all our newly planted trees
just one seemed
destined to disappoint
unlike its decorative brothers
bucketed and shipped
chosen and submerged root-deep
as equals in the same season
this one alone
would not follow suit
and produce as splendid purple leaves
or send out sturdy shoots
to longer reaches

our gardener patience wearing thinner
than its spindly twigs
we settled on an execution date
and even plotted
what to try next thaw of another sort
to more grandly dress the vacant spot

however this quirky winter
  the heavy ice came
  the hard rains fell
  the record spring followed
and after weeks of
head shaking   shrugging
and readying for the last meal
we discovered by sheer accident
that the sapling had never been a sibling
but a shy orphan cousin
of all those plum others
  it had only taken longer
  to embrace its home
  yet was risking far more
  than a picturesque show

    witnessed as if a belated miracle
    the odd adolescent
    was clearly bearing fruit

82 *inexplicable*

i should have been
a better mother

no other failing
grieves me more
than my distractions
as you grew
  the weak attention
  that you knew   while i
  set out to raise my sight
  from self-invented
  destitution

when i hear your laugh today
i know that fortune
has favored me twice

  parents whose abiding affection
  rivals the rarity
  of a blazing comet
  in the bethlehem night

children
whose inexplicable forgiveness
allows me to imagine
having done some small things right

83 channel settings

this view of self-worth
is not avant-garde thinking
for someone so clever
as to have plural degrees
though it is not higher learning
that brought me to my knees
but channel settings disconcertingly akin
    this quid pro quo   pyramid scheme
   haves-have-nots   see-no-evil
  mine-comes-first   elitist   fix we are in

(in paris   i put my face
only inches away
from an emerald embedded dish
touched by the fingers
of marie antoinette's chamber lady
   extravagance as crass
   as revolution was just
some days it is the stars
stretching my grip on infinity
  but greed old or new
  in full bloom boggles too)

it requires no doctorate
in conventional theology
to assess the evidence
and foretell with perfect odds
  that zeus and jehovah and allah and god
are not resubscribing to   *motor trends*
and though in the end we may be our own judge
whether we limp the last mile   or floor a lexus suv
no mortals bow worshipfully to   a   c e o   *of the dead*
  no more do we believe that the kind proceed to hell
(though someone above or below may inquire
whether we listened to our children well   or ever)

84   a melody's lift

    how can it be
    that song moves us so

    or is it music alone
      (rhythms entwined with voice and tone
        first sent aloft
        to float and furrow in new dimensions
          then suspending time
          before seeking departure in resolution)
    that sounds our unique identity

    is any art form more exclusively human

    and then i recall pulling off at a road
    where aspen leaves jingled
    and giant pines sighed
    long grasses whispered
    to skittering squirrels
    a captured wind moaned through the crests of trees
      and a coyote paused to ponder me

    i crooned him a greeting organic and native
      i was pleased i had lent him a melody's lift

    (as a thunder crack scattered me back to my car
      the wild creature stayed to hear beethoven's fifth)

85 *inner fire*

it is easter sunday

the spring has been g o o d
the air is cooler than the average record
   likes to give   these   texas   hills
the soaker hoses
   have been laid and looped
     through the newly planted salvia beds
the rose amaryllis just unveiled itself on cue

it is the perfect day to think of you

and though your ashes were simply strewn
at the water's edge in a distant summer
and the ocean long since swept your dust away
i would still set forth to the world's other edge
through the barbed wire streets near galilee
duck bullets and rocks if i thought i could find
the overgrown garden where a soft rain has fallen
with particles from your hair and your inner fire
to roll aside the counterpoise of passing time
    and find you waiting at the portal there

i would tell you   *s i s t e r*
   back home we are finally growing flowers
and you would respond   as you often did
      today i am going to live

86 reservoirs

it may well be
that there is nothing left
to tell or say
from where we
perspire
on this blue and dust earth
of greater value
or equal worth than
remembrance
  of self-sustaining light
    humbling any sun
of passion for life
    that runs beyond the shallow grave
    into waters
    flowing
    one molecule
    at a time
    from our endless past
    to the spiritual reservoirs
      refilling our liquid future

87 spun

i would not
subscribe
to potions
and crystals
or tarot cards
and star charts
or extra sensory
meteorology
or
a singled out prayer
or a narrow
worship door
with only
one doxology

i have received
too many
answers
to my most
bleak supplication
to think
that anything
i did right or wrong
brought on
this
silk connectedness
to
spun understanding
beyond
my understanding

88 *before goodbye*

in an english town renowned
  for its mills and pottery kilns
  and ravishing petals
  and window boxes
where ecru lace curtains
brush open sills   is a church so old
its metal steeple tilts   as it has
for hundreds of years
as it might well have done
when my own daddy's father's
great-grandfather's father
twice or thrice before that
stared up from a simple pew
and asked for firsthand faith
  that the earth was really round
  that the wooden ship would hold
  that the lathed mast would not splinter
  that fresh water would last and flour would stay dry
  that the waves would not lap
    too much higher than the bow
all this before goodbye and casting off for america
  some stretch of time later   i myself observed
  this green british spot from the wings of a splendid jet
  where eight cramped hours was enough to take its toll
on my pampered and single-fold
sense of self-sacrifice
  but my silver-haired father
  made the homage voyage as well
  and as always my smiling and steadfast mother
  and when these two entered
  and stood in the gray stone chapel
  to nod in deep wonder
  i could not swallow
    i will behold no certitude as polar set or rich
      nor humility i would sail more far to follow

atlantis

i cannot think
what melody
was sung or hummed
or ached as people
lost their sense of land in sight
i cannot bring myself
to guess
what rock to rock
was left behind
and then at once
begun again without
the chance for change of heart

i cannot close my eyes
to conjure
     human cargo
           stacked in hulls
third-reich box-cars   fetid cells
    a newly unearthed
        cache of bones
    and broken skulls

i do not open
this mouth to let it speak
of suffering
or take this pen
and ask it to pretend
it knows
where the soul wanders
when it searches for goodness
    with last hope receding seasons ago
      with nothing but dark and crashing night
          or a crying child's
        pipe dream of a floating atlantis
          altering the horizon

90 *a b u n d a n c e*

april is too soon
for thanksgiving

but when a table
 has been set
before you

    freedom

  peace   love

    beauty

  (even

    purpose

finding its place)

it is not right
to take
living
for granted

to act as if
abundance
adheres to highest merit
 or as if privation were
 a lesser god's
    minor oversight

91 small feet

i believed
when i was waist high
  that birds chuckled over riddles while in flight
  that dandelions called each other's names
  that the elephant eyes in paneled maple
spent evenings kindly studying me
i was certain that layered bedtime covers
hid (down a ladder from an elusive entry)
a wondrous wish-filled fairyland
      that i was not yet wise enough to see
i knew after all on my own in the night
  that the shimmering glow in the winking wind
    was an enormous diamond and not a streetlight
i had also witnessed the vertical departure
  of a plump red balloon
  hardly lost on a string
as a fool's child would have thought
  but buoyed beyond near stars to the far-off moon
and it was i who clung oddly
  to a funny frayed blanket
  making it my not-so-secret talisman
     who hung onto the true-blue panda
     twosey-onesey
since no savage doubt lurked
    only voices soothing
  yes you do   o h y e s you can

here is where innocence should reside
  where treasure glitters on the washed ocean floor
  where small feet follow sprites
     by the sandman's castle
  and jovial dolphins join fins
    to hold back the tides

fraction

how many words are left
  times how many days
    plus how many deeds
their remainder undone
or greater minus commentary
  instead of kinder action spent
if we knew the sum
  of this syntax puzzle
we could subtract our faults
  and lay claim to virtue

i do not think that higher math
makes common dividends more divisible
    self is one prime not a number

  with exponential
    a fraction spirit
disappears
    approaching zero

93 glitches

in this fast-paced *technified* age
our choppy seas are metaphors
all the old evils are obsolete
and were it not for
a few remaining glitches
   (bigotry   decadence   starvation   wars)
   we could go on record
   as the first earthling age
   to achieve perfection

seeing as how
such historic greatness
has been handily corralled
by so-called *h u m a n s*
anyone in the universe can

94 creed

    my mother
    lives among her flowers
    she sees their details
    not as well as she perceives
    their total air or smells their
    rich and subtle scents
    and though she knows
    the needs of species
      (almanac requirements
    water   sun   and prudent weeding)
    she also says their latin names
       as a maker would
       pleased with creation on *the third day*
    so when she carries trowel or hoe
      or wheels fresh compost to a border bed
    i believe her gardens have a creed
     there's more than form to getting fed
       i have watched the exchange
       as she leans her face to theirs
         their mystic syllables   her tender talk
    roses and pentas when she comes
      pronounce for the hummingbirds

    see
       where
              light
                    walks

95 daily bread

    let there be greens
      let there be blues
        and with such rich colors
    earthy browns too

    then all else follows
      every palette
      and perfume
      each artist's inspiration
      as well as daily bread

    and somewhat less obvious
      the substance of the dead
        their sweat and sinew
        their skin and salt

    how more could we exalt their souls
    than to sanctify our air and streams
    and esteem soil fairer far than gold

96 *softy*

   my graying sweetheart
    is taking me to the prom
    we won't look like seniors of the high school kind
      no matter what we might put on
        (together twenty years
           this may be our second date)
he has scoured our jumbled closet
  and unrolled his only tie
while i foraged for fresh stockings
  so to stroll with fewer runs
we succumbed to fleeting panic
  until a strand of leather rope
  proved to be the wardrobe trick
  that would hold his trousers up
then with no true jewels to wear
  i produced a stunning tangle
  of my silver costume bangles
  and a loop of ersatz jade
i have trimmed some wilder hairs
  from the tops of his ears
and doused my own limp locks
  with a sheen of party glow
through this whole peculiar april day
   my enigmatic mate and i have giggled
   at each other as if we never left sixteen
and when my back was turned
  the softy rogue sneaked away to buy
  a pink and lace corsage for pinning him to me

a couple of aging and work-worn teachers
not past preening dress-ups or lessons self-taught in play
(solemnly we pledge to keep the s l o w e r lane
  we shall embark ahead of time
    it is positively dangerous
  to love   and laugh   and drive)

bell tower

across the river
  from where we wait
  to enter the dance
  so that no one will notice
are the high-rise glass-cut
monoliths to corporate class
and profit margins
and fast-track paths
to tidy fortunes

across the evening water
  where the grackles
  skim above lapping waves
  for all-you-can-eat
  insect hors-d'oeuvres
construction cranes sprout up
like crabgrass stalks

across the timeless colorado
  hidden in plain sight
is the same brick bell tower
  that marked history
  thirty years ago
  when i first looked
and now stands holding its ground
  still a monument to an extinct age
    and even though
    the century has turned another page
    and the millennium
  still honoring
    each landmark sixty minutes
  still clanging worthy of anyone's
    first or last hour

98 *butterfly*

who can begrudge
the sputtering of the fuse
  who has stroked
  fingers along
  such flowing current

who can decry
the waning of the light
  who has touched
  sleeping eyelids
  with tears of pride

who can forgo
the attitude of prayer
  who has consumed
  the emptiness
  of a half-filled jar

who can prefer
the static of denial
  who has brushed
  the iridescence
  from a fallen butterfly

who can protest
the closing of a door
  who has flown
  through open windows
  and put small wings to use

99 *bequeathed*

    i would not have to pause
    to name one cherished gift   the material thing
    bestowed upon me   surpassing all
    my private treasury   before and since
      a cardboard box from *granny*
        when i was less than ten   containing ribbons
        and knotted bows   jingling bracelets
        jeweled buttons   squares of bright cloth
        sunday brooches   tatted lace   crocheted doilies
        eyelet hankies   wooden spools   doll dresses
        soft purses delicately decked with beads
    if my grandmother sensed ahead of time
    the worth these artifacts grew to have
    i am still ever glad that i thanked her after
    not once   in my imaginings   but often
    though no other older son's only daughter
    could have been more ostensibly unlike her
      (i   neither skilled with embroidery needles
        nor patient with pulling thread
          meticulous in polishing or gifted in the kitchen
            steadfast as guardian of exotic blossoms
          or gracious at flying piano keys
    my disheveled domain when she came to visit
    stood contrary to any such qualities)
     but our two photographs side by side
     are all the proof an observer needs
     to see that she must have also bequeathed
        her nineteenth-century subdued irish smile

      these plain print poems lacking any o r n a m e n t
      are all i can find of antique joy to offer
      my own grand-nephew or great-granddaughter
        may some few words here bridge our worlds to theirs
        boxed or bound   in humble sight or secret grace
      may they reside among far less sorrow than laughter

100 *page-long*

someone brighter
could suffer
intellectual qualms
from calling
these page-long
epiphanies *psalms*
but it's been known
for a long time
(since before we were born)
that fervor
is all we
can ever
draw on
to convey
our
raison d'être

101 kindred

to paraphrase a kindred soul
i have no will to slander

*when you look for me next
after i have gone
 sit still
 to hear a singular song
 and let it take shape
on the next blank page
 with words neither yours nor mine
 but our own
 the finer threads in heart and voice
 the distance grander than our end*

About the Author

Judith Austin Mills grew up surrounded by music and literature, an upbringing that she says "makes rhythm and rhyme natural friends" to her poetry. She credits family moves during childhood for her appreciation of adventure and contrast. Northern states gave her indelible memories of seasonal change, but settling in Texas made her "dig deep to see beauty in any landscape."

At the University of Texas, she earned her first degree and then years later her M.A. in English with a Creative Writing concentration. She has been writing fiction and poetry ever since, while earning her living as a teacher—frequently in the French classroom. Currently, Judith Austin Mills is an Adjunct Associate Professor of English at Austin Community College.

Her short stories and poems have appeared in diverse publications, including the *Texas Poetry Calendar*. The fiction manuscript *Tripping Home* won a Writers' League of Texas competition in 2001. In 2011, Plain View Press published her historical novel *How Far Tomorrow*, set during the Texas Revolution. She is completing its sequel.

About the Artist

Genie Maples is an established abstract artist living in the Asheville, North Carolina, community. Painting professionally since 2002, she allows the interaction of colors and emotion to drive her work. Her artwork is purchased and exhibited internationally. Genie Maples is the author's cousin.

Gratitude

The author's late father, Gene R. Mills, took time in the spring of 2001 to learn the painstaking steps of book binding. He crafted several hardback versions of this manuscript, which were given as keepsakes to family and friends. No less gratitude goes to the author's mother, Josephine Hunt Mills. Despite low vision and an approaching ninetieth birthday, she helped proofread every page of this eventual 2014 publication. Her words of encouragement are another treasure—"Long life to Danda!"